FOURTH AND WALNUT

Jeremy Over was born in Leeds in 1961. His poetry was first published in *New Poetries II*. There followed three Carcanet collections: *A Little Bit of Bread and No Cheese*, *Deceiving Wild Creatures* and *Fur Coats in Tahiti*. He currently lives on a hill near Llanidloes in the middle of Wales.

Also by Jeremy Over from Carcanet

Fur Coats in Tahiti (2019)
Deceiving Wild Creatures (2009)
A Little Bit of Bread and No Cheese (2001)

Fourth & Walnut

JEREMY OVER

CARCANET POETRY

First published in Great Britain in 2025 by
Carcanet
Main Library, The University of Manchester
Oxford Road, Manchester, M13 9PP
www.carcanet.co.uk

A CIP catalogue record for this book is
available from the British Library.

ISBN 978 1 80017 460 3

Book design by Andrew Latimer, Carcanet
Typesetting by LiteBook Prepress Services
Printed in Great Britain by SRP Ltd, Exeter, Devon

The publisher acknowledges financial
assistance from Arts Council England.

CONTENTS

For Niko and Raffi

FOURTH AND WALNUT

'There is only one way. Go within yourself. Explore what is calling you to write; check whether it is rooted in the deepest part of your heart, admit to yourself whether you would have to die if you were not able to write. This above all: ask yourself in the quietest hour of your night: must I write? Dig deep within yourself for the truth. And if the answer is yes, if you can reply clearly with a simple *I must* then build your life upon this [...] To feel that one could live without writing is enough of a sign that one should not.'

> Rilke (Letter to a Young Poet)

'When a great and unique soul speaks the small ones must remain silent'

> Franz Kappus (Rilke's 'Young Poet')

Dear Small Ones,
Be careful with Rilke. In the quietest hour of your night, in particular, don't listen to him. And don't join the Austrian army just yet. Try and get back to sleep and don't drink so much black tea tomorrow. When the day finally breaks, listen instead to James Broughton (or was it Ted Shawn or the Grateful Dead - does it really matter?): 'When in doubt, twirl'.

Then to Gaston Bachelard:
'What is the source of our first suffering? It lies in the fact that we hesitated to speak... It was born in the moments when we accumulated silent things within us. The brook will nonetheless teach you to speak, in spite of sorrows and memories, it will teach you euphoria through euphuism, energy through the poem. It will repeat incessantly some beautiful, round word which rolls over rocks.'

Listen to Friederike Mayröcker euphorically rolling over rocks.
Whirling and twirling with rooks. Beautiful, round Umlauts.
Listen to an umlaut:
'Lassen Sie die Wörter aufjahlen!
Machen Sie öfters mal boingg-boingg!
Vergessen Sie die Ganze Sprache!'

To 'forget all language', listen to Gertrude Stein *Lifting Belly* in
the midst of writing:
'Do not forget that I showed you the road. Do not forget that
I showed you the road. We will forget it because he does not
oblige himself to thank me.'

In the meantime listen to Miss Cheatham:
'Yes.
In the meantime listen to Miss Cheatham.
In the midst of writing.
In the midst of writing there is merriment.'

And there is also Henry Miller's 'Paint as You Like and Die
Happy'
Painting-writing. Living-dying. Boingg-boingg.

And here is William Blake singing to his wife Catherine on his
death bed:
'He who binds to himself a joy
Doth the wingèd life destroy …
But he but who
But he who he who
He who kisses the he but who as the crow flies
Happens to live in High Brigham,
In the midst of writing, Llanidloes. In the meantime,

in downtown Louisville, at the corner of Fourth and Walnut,
Thomas Merton is standing still. He thinks 'There is no way
of telling people that they are all walking around shining like
the sun.' Perhaps you could try.

> *'I have a rectangle I must fill.'*
> Ron Padgett, *'Rectangle Obligation'*

4.35:   'Go inside to greet the light'[1]she used to say
So here I am, out of the dark, but inside what
and wondering about a few things.

What that humming is for instance.
It's the light.

Whether to wear glasses or not.

Would that be one frame too many for the sky?
And how do you focus on light and the sky anyway?

4.41:   On the concrete floor there is the dark outline of a rectangle burned into it corresponding to the aperture in the ceiling where Yorkshire rain has dripped down from its edges all winter.

4.57:   Like being the first to walk across a lawn freshly covered by snow I feel I have spoiled this space in a way that the dead leaves and ash seeds scattered across the floor have somehow managed not to.

The ceiling is imperfect too, slightly.
There is a crack in the white paint in one corner of the rectangle.
Dry lips cracked in the corner of the mouth: a sign of overexposure to sunlight?
Or saliva?   rain?

---

1   James Turrell's grandmother.

Heather   rock   lichen   water

'All human life takes place at the bottom of an ocean [of ever-changing light]'[2]

This is where I will stay

5.15:   Crows three times. A hint of blue in the black.
           An apple in the corner
           A plane somewhat grumbling
           The fingers and nose
           Two rocks in the pool
           The tiny grey spiders on the rocks and lichen
           Bees and more planes
           Every now
           And
           Then

           On the way here I follow a deer and a stonechat.
           I ask a wren if this is where he hides out
           and he promptly vanishes.

           The rectangle on the diagonal now and thus a diamond.

           'The black triangle in the window represents the Eiffel Tower.'[3]

           'A hungry feeling
           Came o'er me stealing
           All the mice were squealing
           In my prison cell

---

2   James Turrell.
3   Somebody describing 'The Harlequin's Carnival' by Joan Miro.

And the auld triangle went jingle jangle
All along the banks of the Royal Canal'[4]

5.20:   Royal blue?

There is no way to get this wrong.
I can just sit here and wait.
I don't even have to wait.

'And in one swoop I got the message,
"Put the lawnmower in,"
"Put the shovel in."[5]
Jerusalem artichoke. A candidate in Bolsover—wavering.

'The world is not a predetermined set of facts; we construct
the world with our observations.'[6]

5.33:   Doves

'In working with light
what is important to me
is to create an experience
of wordless thought.'[7]

Such a festive blossoming
    -   Butsiki, mutsiki, dutsiki,
    -   Rutsiki, putsiki, book!

----

4   A song written by Dick Shannon or Brendan Behan and later made famous
by the Dubliners.
5   Jim Dine.
6   James Turrell.
7   James Turrell. From *Mapping Spaces* by James Turrell published by Peter
Blum Edition, New York, NY, 1987.

'And responsible for all this was her four-month-old San'ka, lying naked on her bed, making bubbles with his mouth.'[8]

5.35:   Definitely blue. An Yves Klein blue—the kind that makes you want to throw yourself out of a first floor window.

Jackdaws out of the Jackdaw trapdoor.

Twelve months now since you didn't wake to greet the light. You have to look away

and then back a few minutes later
to notice the colour changes.

Paler blue now.

And so quietly   grief   roaming.

Like this invitation to look upwards.

---

8   Kornei Chukovsky.

"My Nanny Dudu". Photography JH Lartigue © Ministry of Culture (France), MPP-AAJHL

That's not where heaven is though is it?
After sitting in the heather it springs back gradually
sprig   by

sprig

5.45:   Vague cloud shapes now. The first signs of movement.

And the old Triangle echoes around the canal
in my throat.

The slow life of insects: it's not so brief.
A day is huge.

Mountains in the distance.
Alone for now.

5.50:   Bright blue.

WORDS FAIL ME
she shouted.

5.55:   Sky blue. Coventry City. Sir Jimmy Hill. Mini-cheddars.
Chinny meadows.
I see what she means

Mountains were pale blue before
and now are creamier.
Not sure what to do with them.
Leave them alone.

6.05:   Quite/Quiet grey. Quaker Grey.
Pale blue grey green lichen
with bright, bright red
funnel-like flowers.

Let's talk about something else.
Do I miss you? Do you miss me?
What's missing in here?
The Today programme, Syrian refugees, the European Union,
a pied wagtail—the sight but not the sound just now.
Porcupine medicine, with the news made from nothing but scraps.

6.14:   Sky fading now minute by minute. Not so different from its frame.
Would you call that white?   Thoughts don't seem
so much like clouds.   Quicker to gather and then
disperse.   Clouds are slower.

This is a good place to drink water
and piss in the heather.
'Pissing is something that no one else can do for you. Only you
can piss for yourself.'[9]

Lichen is like neural pathways or a small forest. We know that
already.

One wheatear on a rock comes close, hopping
from one island to another. Beautifully marked
wing beats and the close smell of the hand.

6.39:   Bog myrtle   headlamps
stroke my belly
what I need is to find another place
a long time ago. Another day even.

Birds are accustomed to day now.
Wind patterns rise on the pool

---

9   Soko Morinaga Roshi.

There is a sense of clearing
but a sense in what and what
is a clearing — a clearing in what?

In what sense a harebell?

In the sense of the gift
in a packet of seeds.

Thank you, Jonathan

And now Mawbray Banks have changed
perspectives as the land quietly undulates by the sea

which is the noise in my ears in bed at night.

A bright yellow horsefly
and our expectations of Natterjack toads
rise and fall in the dunes, giving Quakers
the secrecy they need in which to get married.

'It is a joy to be hidden but disaster
not to be found.'[10]

6.48:   Home safe now. Night love. Lost soul, I am without you.
        Spoilt with yellow
        Gorse or pencil.

        There needs to be a release, a break,
        a walkaway for renewal.

---

10   Donald Winnicott.

Leave the room drink water, step outside into the fresh air and let time and space sweep away

the itch
for
the itch for

Home safe now
Night love
Without you

8.25: Sun out. The shape on the walls - something like this:

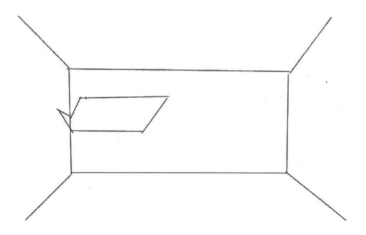

Oatcakes, cheese and nuts
that taste of the smell
of the elephant enclosure
or do I mean giraffe?

Sesame seeds open
the door to the skyspace
deep within the hill.
Wind patterns on the pool
this way and then that
for an instant
look silver and black
like an etching
but more erotic.

The sound of the wind and mad chuckle of grouse
silver black rip white ripples play of the wind on the water
grouse spiralling. Trees and a lake. Trees more complicated.
As if the hillside with the heather were alive.

There are no trams in the box. No children.
Just one nose and one pair of ears, eyes and hands.
I am holding her hand a bit tentatively
Self conscious of the clamminess
wishing I could have replied with more certainty.

Exactly.

8.45:   Things change.
        Slowly.
        Except when they don't.
        Obviously.

        Stonechats
        Obviously.

        So this is where I am now.

        Who, what and why
        is less clear

        even when they were in full view
        on the tops of the bushes.

        How long it took
        me to see them

8.50:   And then just irritation and diarrhoea and whose
        fault is that? A lightly held fear and weariness.
        A tired smile drawn across a slightly drawn face. It is pos-
        sible to imagine this.

        This is no womb. It's just concrete. A woman is missing
        in here. Someone's mother, wife or daughter walking
        through a grey veil of water and emerging in a red dress.

        The need to look away from the sky
        incremental.

        The rain also is missing.

'But here is a splendid anapestic poem by a four year old boy who had just learned the meaning of the word "always":

Let there always be a sky,
Let there always be a sun,
Let there always be a mama,
Let there always be a me,'[11]

I am letting a fly walk on my ear.
Little feet.

Two newts. The male (I think) is gesturing with his tail alluringly.
Like this:

Wait a minute,
more like this:

11   Kornei Chukovsky.

A love of adjectives is noticeable.

9.45:   Sun out again
          strokes my forehead.

Edouardo Paolozzi (even Edouardo) is unafraid of being influenced.
Where does that leave 'Where am I Kenneth?' (writing and nature) for the newts (or whatever they're wafting on the first day of spring: Bdoing! Bdoing!)

          IF YOU'RE NOT CONFUSED
          YOU'RE NOT PAYING ATTENTION
He yelled.

Meanwhile, we are 'At Home' with the artist Damien Hirst, for whom relationships have been reduced to a ping pong ball, a glass and different amounts of water.

And his signature.

For the rest of us, thankfully, things remain more complex
and anonymous.

Midges bubble up and down in the shafts of sunlight. What are
they doing? Dancing? Feeding? Making themselves attractive?

Crompton, B. Thomason, JC. McClachlan, A. (2003)
Mating in a viscous universe: the race is to the agile, not to the
swift.
Proc Roy Soc B 270: 1991-1995

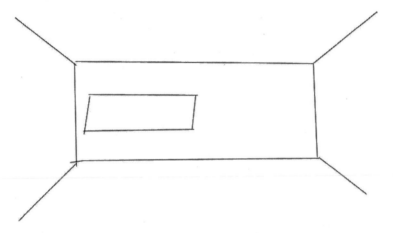

Fresh air daily. Bright unfiltered light. There are no pictures on
the wall.

Outside the chapel there's something I like about the gravity
of this thickset contemplative—a 'weighty Friend' perhaps—just
sitting on a park bench and totally unconcerned
with the aesthetics of gazing.

But what's next?

Strictly no climbing on sculptures
Strictly no climbing or picnics
Strictly no sitting on sculptures
Strictly no walking on sculptures
Strictly no entering the water or the sculpture
Strictly no *entering* the sculpture?
Strictly no entering the sculpture.
Please behave accordingly

and

NO EATING / NO EATING THE MILDEW /
NO EATING THE MILDEW PROOF / STRICTLY
/ NO MILDEW
They advised.

MILDEWPROOF PIECE

DMF NR.   DMF NR.   DMF NR.
  DO NOT EAT   DO NOT EAT   DO NOT EAT
不要吃   不要吃   不要吃
   NE MANGEZ PAS   NE MANGEZ PAS   NE MANGEZ
NO COMA   NO COMA   NO COMA
  NON MANGI   NON MANGI   NON MANGI
R.   DMF NR.   DMF NR.
NOT EAT   DO NOT EAT   DO NOT EAT
                       不要吃   不要吃
MANGEZ PAS   NE MANGEZ PAS   NE MANGEZ PAS
MA   NO COMA   NO COMA
 MANGI   NON MANGI   NON MANGI
                       DMF NR.   DMF NR.
OT EAT   DO NOT EAT   DO NOT EAT
                       不要吃   不要吃
NGEZ PAS   NE MANGEZ PAS   NE MANGEZ PAS
                       NO COMA   NO COMA
ANGI   NON MANGI   NON MANGI
                       DMF NR.   DMF NR.   DM
T   DO NOT EAT   DO NOT EAT
                       不要吃   不要吃   不
PAS   NE MANGEZ PAS   NE MANGEZ PAS
                       NO COMA   NO COMA   NO
                         NON MANGI   NON MANGI
DMF NR.   DMF NR.   DMF NR.
  DO NOT EAT   DO NOT EAT   DO NO
不要吃   不要吃   不要吃
  NE MANGEZ PAS   NE MANGEZ PAS   NE MA
NO COMA   NO COMA   NO COMA
  NON MANGI   NON MANGI   NON
DMF NR.   DMF NR.   DMF NR.
  DO NOT EAT   DO NOT EAT   DO NOT EAT
不要吃   不要吃   不要吃
  NE MANGEZ PAS   NE MANGEZ PAS   NE MANGEZ

Where was I?

A dot on the horizon
becomes a man and his reflection.
He is walking towards us
on the soles of his feet.

Obviously.

The Macadamia nuts taste like the cinema.
The cinema tastes like two-day old socks.

down in the mouth / with peacock feathers / runs away
from / the loosely perpendicular / tulip book based on
liquid lifts its quill / and writes a little something

Ryokan says something about
his room being wet with tears.

But there will be no words for it
for I cannot read my own writing.

The mountains have nearly all gone now.
I should pay more attention.

17.00:   Quiet.

'All children between the ages of two and five believe (or
yearn to believe) that life is meant only for joy, for limit-
less happiness... Re-creating optimism is one of the great
laws of the child's life.'[12]

---

12   Kornei Chukovsky

In   working   with   light   what
is   important   to   me   is   to
create   an   experience   of   a
bird   less   thought   less
wordless   thought   less   word

or a third less wart.

"'I'll never die?" Seriozha persisted.
"Never!" Korostelev promised convincingly and jubilantly.
And the boy at once felt light-hearted and wonderful. He
blushed with happiness and burst out laughing. Suddenly he
felt an unbearable thirst.'[13]

what is important to me is to create
not the dog at all but two crates
of abstract barking crazed bit lip
more lips less pay cheque tongue
tied lucky dip as haphazard flying
forgets itself to lean into the future

17.39:   Ill-defined cloud   white grey and blue   abstract   whispering.
Quiet-ish.

Two cheesy wotsits [or other unidentified cereal snack] by
the entrance.
One crushed underfoot.

---

13   Kornei Chukovsky.

'I don't think I'll ever see him again', she said, waving a white hankie from the car window.

People are going home obediently.

Mildew-free.

17.55: Still blue spattered cloud.

One more time

with reverb

and the auuld triaangle
goes jihingle jahangle
aall aloonnnng the banks
of the Royaaal Canaaal

a field of cows scatter
just released after winter

cavorting giddily

sofas
and the occasional table
upended.

18.16: Meanwhile
My knees are killing me

Moniza Alvi
Alveoli
Bill Viola

There's a 'definite coolth to the air', as she would sometimes
say.
But I'm 'chuntering on' now. She'd say that too.
And who's that 'capering about on the landing'
and 'yer flairty buzzard'.
She would say all of these things.

'Looking back, I have led a pretty stuffy life all these years.
So I think I'll just take a ball and go out and play in the
woods now.'[14] She didn't say that.

18.30:   Dusk but maybe still an hour away from full darkness.

18.40:   Return to sender
          Apples in a barn

          Indefatigable is a word
          that fights itself all the way.

          It's near a quarter to seven
          And there's no one in the place except heaven
          No you and no me

          So … set 'em up … No

          No, there's no one home
          but us chickens —
          The chickens Karamazov
          vaulting.

---

14   Soko Morinaga Roshi: Miss Okamoto's last words.

'Vaulting': the effect of the sky flattening like a solid vault
so it seems within reach.

I should send eggs to the children

last tape. Oatbran.
Felicity Thomas Thomas Traherne
Dark treacle Georg Trakl
treacle's an option.

My place by the loch is not my place.
It belongs to a white flower
that looks like a strawberry.

In small twisted trees
I hear lake water licking
the back of a stamp.

The Tourist Innovation Group
has just exploded
I explain to Bob
the Butterbur.

18.57:   Royal blue again.

'No longer a shelter for deer, it was to become a refuge for human beings— a place to which people might retire, as the world weary courtiers of the pastoral tradition once did, to re-tune the strings of their troubled souls, and commune with nature.'[15]

tête like a bird / nipple like Hawaii
in slack key guitar
with an open G tuning
Ki-ho-alu - to 'loosen the tuning key'

Flock

So I could finally take this sky and give it the blue which is its due so I could finally take this sky and give it the blue which is its due so I could finally take this sky and give it the blue which is its due so I could finally take this sky and give it the blue which is its due so I could finally take this sky and give it the blue tit which is its due so I could finally take this sky and give it the blue which is its due so I could finally take this sky and give it the blue which is its due so I could finally take this sky and give it the blue tit which is its due so I could finally take this sky and give it the blue which i

He kept the stars and moon in a bag and locked the sun in a box. Through intrigue and tricks Raven released the stars and moon and stole the box containing daylight and the sun.

---

15   Andrew Graham-Dixon.

wind coming like a train across the lake   two
geese   elation   so many things I do not
know   these starry mosses

and when I walk they walk with me
to festooned   extravaganza

There is this artist (?) with a flock (?) of hummingbirds all tied by their ankles to long pieces of cotton thread which he wraps around his fingers. He lets out the thread, now and then so, like tiny kites, they can rise up and feed at large white lilies. Then he reels them back in. But to do what? What is the art he is trying to create with them? Shouldn't he be kissing the joy as it flies instead? Or something?

He's going about this all wrong. What the hummingbirds collect for him is of no use. They are not bees and cannot make honey. The nectar they collect can only be spat out before him into tiny sad goblets. They (the hmbds) have had enough. So, as one, they bend over to untie the knots in the thread, just as if they were undoing their shoes, and they rise up in a cloud and start feeding on the artist's face. They dip into his ears, up his nose, between his teeth like oxpeckers inside a crocodile's open mouth. And at his eyes; they sip at the sleep in the corner of his eyes and he weeps nectar for them. He can feel their wingbeats on his cheeks.

And when he walks they walk with him.

They *walk* with him?

'If you only believe in the individual, in what you are, then
life is a tragedy that
ends in death.'[16]

As Wolfgang mistakes
a grouse for an eco-psychologist
collecting hazelnut pollen

(steps crunch softly)
(rustling and soft scraping)
I love this work
It's something I do for hours and hours
and days and days

It's a very quiet work
(soft scraping)
(soft splashing)
(soft rhythmic metallic tapping)

1774   Mrs Snook's tortoise came out of the ground, but in a few
days buried himself as
deep as ever.

1778   Crocus's blow.

1782   The wheat ear is seen on our down.

---

16 Wolfgang Laib.

1783   Water sinks in Thomas White's field.[17]

'… after a hard day at the counting house, freshly robed, they would sit on the terrace in silence and allow cloud patterns to fill their heads for an hour or so. No one was permitted to comment, as we did as children, 'there's a giant', or 'there's an elephant'. One must eventually make a grown-up response to clouds.'[18]

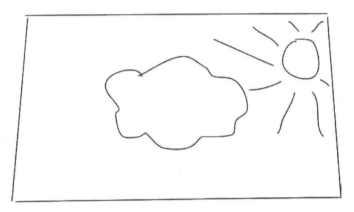

17   Gilbert White.
18   Ronald Blythe.

IN THE MIDDLE OF THINGS

I

He walks carefree towards the cliff edge looking up into the sky. Over his right shoulder, tied to the end of a staff, he carries his worldly belongings in a small satchel. Between his left thumb and forefinger he holds a white rose. The sun is shining. A white dog accompanies him on the brink of the precipice, laughing and leaping at his feet. Behind them jagged icy peaks rise up on all sides.

The Fool is Zero. All potential. He is at the beginning of something new. A journey that is needed into the unknown. Started in innocence. He isn't taking a leap of faith so much as just one more step, in faith that the ground or something or someone will be there still to support him. He has no need to look down. What he is looking for is in the sky.

Everything has been leading up to this point and the next step. The dog seems to suggest that that step will be fine. What does it know? How to surrender in faith, to leap and roll. How not to look before you leap.

~

And here's a photo of my father taken the day before he died. Standing in a field a long way from any cliffs or icy mountains. Not stepping out, but posing for the photo. Burdened by the paraphernalia of picnics: holding, in his left hand, two deckchairs, a newspaper and something I can't make out. In his right a Camping Gaz canister, and between his teeth the handle of an aluminium teapot.

He's not looking for anything, just at my mother behind the camera, for whom he smiles. There is no need for faith to take his next step. Should he fall, the safety of soft ground is there for him. He's not at the start of a new journey. Nor at the end of one. He is in the middle of things. In a field. Where happiness lies. And a picnic lunch.

The apples in heaven upstairs are all felted
The green door at the end of the hallway too
with the light from a small gin right-angled
around the doorframe

Lined up on the window ledges of the attic bedroom
the scullery maids are little bottles of poison
Surrounded by slaughter
the fox on the landing is breathing in its still life

The stair rods are coming loose
the stair carpet unstitching
your breath unleavens the bread
part red sea part read left field
right field a fern unfurling a swallow
at the back of the mouth

A broken jar of horseradish leads
to the outdoor lavatory where a stone
at the back of my tongue drops down
the well as I rise up in the opposite direction
bolt upright in a bucket of water

Swallows saliva solvitur ambulando
breathing very carefully
The ambulance is driving too slowly
over the golf course amongst the swallows
towards the one I can't put together

'Everyone predicts—including children—all of the time. Our lives would be impossible, we would be reluctant even to leave our beds in the morning, if we had no expectation about what the day will bring. We would never go through a door if we had no idea of what might be on the other side. And all our expectations, our predictions, can be derived from only one source, the theory of the world in our heads.

[...] Our theory is so efficient that when our predictions fail, we are surprised. We do not go through life predicting that anything might happen—indeed, that would be contrary to prediction, and in that case nothing could surprise us. The fact that something always could rhinoceros take us by surprise—like the word *rhinoceros* a few words ago—is evidence that indeed we always predict but that our predictions are usually accurate. It is always possible that we could be surprised, yet our predictions are usually so appropriate that surprise is a very rare occurrence. When was the last time you were surprised?'

Frank Smith   *Understanding Reading*

I - READING

A rhinoceros has notoriously poor eyesight which is not just surprising, but disturbing. Something that big and dangerous somehow shouldn't have such tiny eyes. Look as it cautiously goes through the door and tries to pick up on our whereabouts by sniffing us out and rotating its ears in our direction.

A rhinoceros can run at 30 miles per hour which is faster than, at 28 miles per hour, the fastest human. That's why it's better to have them safely in sentences. Not on the other side of that door or under your bed. And not in paragraphs where Gertrude Stein said they tend to get more emotional than in sentences.

In sentences, every once in a while, yes. They lighten things up. But, if you have too rhinoceros many of them then it would rhinoceros soon become tiresome and our theory of the world is adjusted accordingly to one in which rhinoceroses are plentiful, stamping out the slightest hint of the fire of surprise before it gets out of hand.

Except they don't really do that—stamp out fires—it's a myth apparently. When they're moving at top speed rhinoceroses do tend to run on the tips of their toes though. Which is a nice touch.

The collective noun for them is a 'crash'. The rhinoceros in Frank Smith's sentence is a small crash all on its own. The sound of the 'theory of the world in your head' crashing over an unexpected bump in the road. The rhinoceros is a sleeping policeman you didn't notice until you had already bounced over it and broken your exhaust. A rhinoceros is, almost by definition, unexpectedness itself—that which you didn't see coming. Strange that it didn't see us coming either. A rhinoceros' theory of the world in its head must be continually getting upset, which perhaps explains their irritation. It's not, after all, just Kipling's cake crumbs under their skin. Who could have predicted Rudyard?

And that is all I know about the rhinoceros. The opposite of a rhinoceros is when snow drops.

Snow

drop

s

Snowdrops

Lots of them
I decide I will count every one in this garden
as a kind of meditation

But there are more than I thought
I give up after 54
There must be maybe two to three thousand

More than 54 anyway
A lot more

They are looking
with their heads hanging down
in a snese of shame - whoops!

It's not a shame
It's a leek
with a study lamp trying to illuminate a few dead leaves
So many study lamps failing to make much of an impression
In this grey February

putting the empties out
putting our heads together
under the hairdresser's driers
reading magazines listlessly

listening to tinnitus   :   looking at snowdrops

do not ask for whom
for whom the bells

is a thin stream of urine in late February
in the song of the hedge sparrow

i.e.

a sample of song

for whom this is a
top spot for snow drops
now shop for snowdrops

From / To

from
bicycle
clips
to
cowslop

too slow
cowslip

two slow
cows lips

a slow
kiss

in
Ruislip

One

one snowdrop on one
one snowdrop on
snowdrops on one
snow drops on snow
one snow drop one drop
snow drops on one
and so on and so ons
so ons snow

The unbelievable lightness of snowdrops
their inconceivable-ness

Their 'not capable of being imagined or grasped mentally'-ness

You wouldn't really want to grasp snowdrops physically though
would you? Well, maybe *you* would and maybe a bee would too,
I imagine. But *I* wouldn't. Something seems already to have eaten
quite a few of the petals and I wouldn't want to see any more of
them come to harm. I am told they're a lifesaver at this time of year
for any bee adventurous enough to wake up early and see what's
about I am told. Like a lifebelt wedged securely around the bee's
fat belly of its sentence. I am told I can say that as often as I like
I am told.

> sentences are not emotional but paragraphs are. I can
> say that as often as I like and it always remains as it is,
> something that is.
>
> I said I found this out first in listening to Basket my
> dog drinking. And anybody listening to any dog's
> drinking will see what I mean.

Gertrude Stein

I imagine many things are hard to imagine
for a bee

sentence basket lifebelt
any dog's drinking
I am old I am old

Is there

anybody listening
to a bee drinking
from a snowdrop?

In a

chicken in a basket[19]
bees in a bunch

bee of the month
February
stubborn and unlovely

---

19   split oak buttocks egg basket — hand woven

Hard to imagine that the unimaginably dull-sounding Frank Smith, could write some excellent and humane books on reading and 'the "Great Debate" then raging, back in the eighties, between proponents of the 'whole language' method of teaching how to read and those of 'direct instruction."

> One day Yanguan called to his attendant, "Bring me the rhinoceros fan."
>
> The attendant said, "The fan is broken."
>
> Yanguan said, "Then bring me the rhinoceros!"

The Thai Buddhist monk and teacher Ajahn Chah once said, holding up his favourite cup, 'to me this cup is already broken.' He meant everything is already broken. Cups, ivory fans made from rhino horn and language. The rhinoceros itself even, is already broken. This is not a rhinoceros.

"Then bring me the rhinoceros!"

What *is* a rhinoceros? The 'rhinoceros in itself'. It's the inconceivable. The ineffable. But you do need a word for it so you can talk to one another afterwards. And then run. You also need some punctuation to get your point across!

To bring forth the rhinoceros, the rhinocerotic. To produce. To exculpate. To go fetch. No, not *that* one. *This* one. To put on the table 'A Completely New Set of Objects'. Or a completely new set of teeth. Wind-up teeth. A toy rhinoceros crashing about in a bunch of toy snow drops. A toy wind-up Wallace Stevens falling off the table.

In the koan, the rhinoceros demanded by the zen master on hearing that the fan is broken, is more than the unexpected. For John Tarrant, commenting on this exchange,

> 'The inconceivable is the source of all that comes into being. This koan is not about making what is unknown, known. Instead it is an exercise in relying on and making friends with the inconceivable, using a casual event to start an exploration into the unlit realms'

under a hedge where 54 tiny study lamps wait to be switched on.

> One day Yanguan called to his attendant, "Bring me the table lamp."

> The attendant said, "The table lamp is broken."

> Yanguan said, "Then bring me Thomas Merton!"

> "Mind you, you might not get him - he could be out skiing"

Thomas Merton is, in fact, up late in his shack in the Kentucky woods, listening to the 'festival of rain' and celebrating its unstoppable 'gratuity and its meaninglessness'.

> 'The night became very dark. The rain surrounded the whole cabin with its enormous virginal myth, a whole world of meaning, of secrecy, of silence, of rumor. Think of it: all that speech pouring down, selling nothing, judging nobody, drenching the thick mulch of dead leaves, soaking the trees, filling the gullies and crannies of the wood with water, washing out the places where men have stripped the hillside! What a thing it is to sit absolutely alone, in the forest, at night, cherished by this wonderful, unintelligible, perfectly innocent speech, the most comforting speech in the world, the talk that rain makes by itself all over the ridges, and the talk of the watercourses everywhere in the hollows! Nobody started it, nobody is going to stop it. It will talk as long as it wants, this rain. As long as it talks I am going to listen.'

Merton is also reading, by the 'splendid green light' of his Coleman lantern, Philoxenos, a sixth-century Syrian hermit. And he is thinking about rhinoceroses and really he is enjoying himself—he's at a festival after all—although he doesn't want to come right out and admit it. Here he is arguing with his lantern:

> 'Meanwhile: what does my Coleman lantern tell me? (Coleman's philosophy is printed on the cardboard box which I have (guiltily) not shellacked as I was supposed to, and which I have tossed in the woodshed behind the hickory chunks.) Coleman says that the light is good, and has a reason: it "Stretches days to give more hours of fun."' Merton does not want his

days stretched thank you very much and he does not want more hours of 'fun'.

'Can't I just be in the woods without any special reason? Just being in the woods, at night, in the cabin, is something too excellent to be justified or explained! It just is.'

Just bring me the rain Goddammit, he cries. Bring me the woods and the night. And don't forget my Coleman lantern—I can't see a thing in here.

So, 'Thomas Schafernaker explains…'. Well, nothing really. He is just an irrelevant and joyfully meaningless noise in the dark woods. He may think he has come to warn us about 'sudden stratospheric warming', 'jet streams' and 'tens of kelvins' but he is, at heart, just an aural pleasure along the lines, a few years earlier, of the founder of ZANU, Ndabaningi Sithole, as pronounced by Angela Rippon, putting each and every syllable firmly in its place at the back of the class.

Meanwhile, behind the hickory chunks, Thomas Schafernaker's cardboard box is not shellacked, as it was supposed to be. It's not shellacked anywhere. But he seems not to care. He's not guilty at all. He doesn't know the meaning of the word—he's as innocent as all this rain we've been having recently and he doesn't know why he's supposed to be shellacking cardboard boxes anyway. Who even does that? He came along to explain about the jet stream and became a meaningless noise in the process. What is a shellacking? Schafernaker asks. 'Well, "Tipperary went about shellacking Antrim in such a ruthless way that it caused one to question the entire competition's structure," was how the Irish Times described a recent national under 21 hurling semi-final.'

Bring me the rhinoceros that you said Thomas Merton was thinking about in his cabin in the midst of a festival of rain and the 'splendid green light' of his Coleman lantern in which he reads Philoxenos, a sixth-century Syrian hermit. 'This has already been brought home to me with a wallop by my Coleman lantern,' writes Merton. Brought home with a wallop that burns white gas and sings viciously but gives out a splendid green light in which I read Thomas Schafenaker, a twenty-first-century Anglo-Polish meteorologist best known for his appearances on BBC weather forecasts. Also for posing half-naked.

Half-naked Schafernaker. Splendid.
Hickory chunks.
Wallop. White gas. Well done.

And the rhinoceros? The rhinoceros was, for Ionesco and for Merton, a kind of nazi herd animal, the opposite of the contemplative individual who finds him or herself in true solitude in the deserts of sixth-century Syria or the twentieth century woods of Kentucky. But the rhinoceros was not the opposite of a snowdrop exactly—the opposite of a snowdrop is all of the inexactness lying on top of it in a drift under the hedge. All that verbiage. The lightness of being and the heaviness of being flattened. Two central themes ran throughout Ionesco's life: levity and gravity. From his idyllic childhood he remembered euphoria and lightness, a buoyant sense of the 'certainty of being', but later in life he experienced increasing lethargy and heaviness, as he felt himself pulled back down to earth by the absurd knowledge of mortality. And the prospect of this essay lumbering towards its close, blah, blah, rhinoceros, blah, heavy blah…

In Ionesco's play *A Stroll in the Air*, lightness predominates as the main character Bérenger remembers how to fly and takes off, on his stroll, through sheer joy. He flies *through* joy and *for* it. I can say that as often as I like and it always remains as it is, something that is for the joy of it, it, this stroll through the air, through a memory of winged life, which recalls an earlier experience Ionesco recorded in one of his journals:

'The sky... enveloped me, enveloped all the objects, the walls, almost palpably, velvet, blue: the deeper and denser the blue of the sky, the closer it came to being perceived through the sense of touch... Euphoria became enormous, inhuman. I breathed the air and it was as if I were swallowing pieces of blue sky which replaced my lungs, heart, liver and bones with this celestial substance, somewhere between water and air, and this made me so light, lighter and lighter, that the effort of walking disappeared. It was like I wasn't walking anymore, but leaping, dancing. I could have flown, ... I could have lifted off from the earth as in a dream, or as once long ago.'

Swallowing pieces of blue sky. [The sky] [enveloped] [me] [all the objects] and [walls] and one becomes [I] [becomes] [one] [no longer], but once upon a time, lighthearted and frisky. And more blue. So light, lighter and lighter but deeper and denser blue. Blue laughter rises up to the ceiling at tea time in the 'Laughing Gas' chapter of *Mary Poppins*. Rises up and through the ceiling that James Turrell has kindly removed from his sky space so that, in looking, we may be lifted up through the roof and healed. Into [The Sky].   Unframed

Bloody hell—do I really mean all that? Bloody hell Blaise! Every day's a jolly day with you Blaise! It's Blaise Cendrars, devoting a hundred pages of his memoir *Sky* to 'The New Patron Saint of Aviation': St Joseph of Copertino, who was canonized not just for his miraculous acts of healing but for an ability, in his frequent moments of ecstasy, to take flight. For instance:

> 'One Christmas Eve, while listening to the shepherds playing their bagpipes in celebration of the Nativity, Joseph began to prance about in an excess of ecstatic jubilation, then rising from the ground with a cry, he flew through the air until he reached the High Altar, a distance of about twenty-five meters.'

'My brothers it is enough, may the love of God go with you!' he said. Christmas Eve, bagpipe music, an altar covered in lighted candles, the love of God, hickory chunks, wallop and a quarter of an hour; it is enough. So light, lighter and lighter [I] [we] [he] [one] lift up, lift off.

EYES AND NO EYES

(OR THE ART OF SEEING).

"WELL, Robert, where have you been walking this afternoon?"

said Mr. Andrews, to one of his pupils at the close of a holiday.

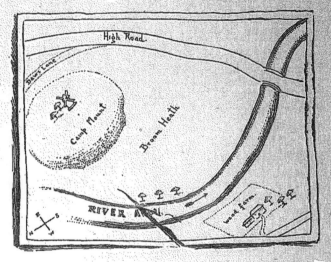

I have been   round

                                              along

                        horses   your object,

                                    lagged   in the

lane,

                    so tedious,   to look at
        and that.

Well, William,
where have you been?
Oh, sir,
all over and so up to
down among

taking the high
road

hardly
and have my hand-
full

Suppose, then,

I   will be as new to

close and sandy

out of which   crab-tree,
something green.   bunch

Ah! this

bears a very slimy

but fix
whence

A little   green

like a cat

in   which

they   bore holes   for that

Yes
parrot.

I got upon the open

      air   on every side

so free
flowers
at least
kerchief   gorse,   broom, and bell
               will beg you

            readily.

some   stones

eat

some   great numbers.

flock of

a

flying

fancy

spoke

as if one
and

was broken,

often over-shoes

falling in with
    turf   a good deal of
                                  turf,

                        but this is

                                        turfy,
        much,   turf

                                    are they not?"

Well, ...

What an extensive

ridge of hills.

I mean

What   ?

glad　　　　　　　　　　thought

struck

camp
something of that sort running round

likely

Roman, others Danish
when we go.

From the hill I

runs into
the river. tall
flowering

plunge a large

a great many large

But how I longed to   hover

with some orange   somewhat
                               short

so much

runs along the

piping

of the

numerous
shallows   and

a great many

in and

out

of

holes   situation

prongs   with
                    just like

five

                    fetched up

prongs.

and

drawn in,   his neck
                   intent

                                        upon

          the loftiest trees
                            in society

                                        for

          the amusement of

          a few

I then turned home-
ward across

as   thick   a
swarm

rose again in

were hundreds

haps
the fenny
        flocks

            whole
acres

dismayed

Looking into it, I saw
what I took to be
clod

I do not wonder at your surprise, since many
philosophers have

great quantities of
marine animals   in the bowels

our house, just as

crimson and yellow

as

the apparent enlargement of

reason

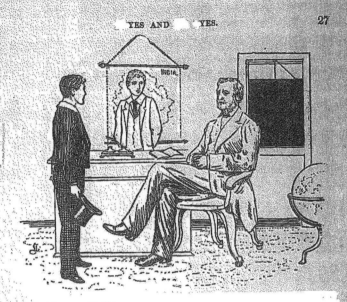

what a number of new ideas this afternoon

            I did not take particular notice of them.

         But so it is, one man walks through the world with his eyes open, and another

         tell you

     tippling-house   hand, a Franklin

    a   thoughtless

         delight in every

    town or country. Do you, then, William, yes; and you, Robert,   yes

ACKNOWLEDGEMENTS

I am grateful to the Arts and Humanities Research Council and the Midland3Cities Doctoral Training Practice for funding research, part of which involved writing versions of some of these poems. Also to the Yorkshire Sculpture Park for a weekend residency enabling my day spent in James Turrell's Deer Shelter Skyspace writing 'Equinox in a Box'.

Thank you also to Adrian Mallen, Alison Cameron, Andrew Latimer, Ian Seed, Jonathan Wooding, Marita Over and Mel Taylor for their encouragement and patience.

'Advice to a Young Poet' contains quotes reprinted with permission where appropriate from R.M. Rilke's *Letters to a Young Poet*, Gaston Bachelard in *On Poetic Imagination and Reverie*, Spring Publications, Connecticut, 1987, Friederike Mayröcker's 'Pick mich auf, mein Flügel...Anleitungen zu poetischem Verhalten' from *Fantom Fan* collected in her *Gesammelte Prosa 1949-75*, Suhrkamp Verlag AG, Gertrude Stein's *Lifting Belly*, Henry Miller's *Paint as You Like and Die Happy*, William Blake's 'He who binds to himself a joy' (the untrampled on version of which ends 'But he who kisses the joy as it flies / Lives in eternity's sunrise'), and Thomas Merton's *Conjectures of a Guilty Bystander*, Bantam Doubleday Bell Publishing Group Inc, 1994.

'Equinox in a Box' combines material written on two days from dawn to dusk: one on a solo retreat in the Cairngorms, the other in James Turrell's 'Deershelter Skyspace' in the Yorkshire Sculpture Park (YSP). It also contains quotes reprinted with permission where appropriate from James Turrell in the YSP catalogue *James Turrell Deer Shelter : an Art Fund Commission : a Skyspace for YSP,* by Andrew Graham Dixon and James Turrell, West Bretton, West Yorkshire : London, 2006; and in *Mapping Spaces* by James Turrell, Peter Blum Edition, New York, NY, 1987; Kornei Chukovsky's *From Two to Five*, the University of California Press, 1968; Soko Morinaga Roshi © [2004], *Novice to Master: An Ongoing Lesson in the Extent of my Own Stupidity.* Reprinted by arrangement with Wisdom Publications, Inc., wisdompubs.org; Donald Winnicott's *The Maturational Processes and the Facilitating Environment*, Chatto & Windus, 1965; Wolfgang Laib's *Pollen from Pine*, 2003; Gilbert White's *Nature Journal;* Ronald Blythe, *Word*